Dream Houses

Dream Houses

Tessa Sinclair Scott

© 2019 Tessa Sinclair Scott. All rights reserved. This material may not be reproduced in any form, published, reprinted, recorded, performed, broadcast, without the express written consent of Tessa Sinclair Scott. All such actions are strictly prohibited by law.

Cover Design: Tessa Sinclair Scott
Cover Image: Hypnos, British Museum Catalogue No. 267, 1915, British Museum. Dept. of Greek and Roman Antiquities; Walters, Henry Beauchamp, 1867-1944. P.D.U.S

ISBN: 978-1-949229-84-4

Kelsay Books
Aldrich Press
www.kelsaybooks.com

For Theo and Andrés.

Acknowledgments

Thank you to these people who supported the elephantine gestation of this collection with insight, faith and humour. In particular; *Lubi Barre, Judith Beveridge, Rebecca Garron, Jonis Hartmann, Jeremy Allan Hawkins, Janet Kenny, Adrian Lăcătuș, Andra Rotaru, Elisabeth Rudolf, the Scott Whanau, Andrés Crump Schnurbusch, Tiggy Weißer, Ina Wolf-Bauwens, and the Hamburg Writers' Group.*

The poems in this collection have been presented in various forms for *Fractalia*, *Crevice*, *AHAB Reading Series*, *Hafenlesung Reading Series*, and the *European Poetry Biennale*, at the Transilvania University of Brașov.

Contents

Dream Houses

Dream Houses	17
Green House	19
Purblind	21
On Arthur Street, in Onehunga	22
The Zigzag Girl	23
Now, tower	24
Secret Life of Stuff	25
Sea Wall	26
A is for Aviator	27
Burj Khalifa	28

Paradise Diptych

Paradise Diptych	31
The Valley	32
Pine Cone Owls	33
The Milky Way from the Veggie Patch	34
A Baumhaus is a Treehouse	35
Jenny's Honey Shed	36
Notes on Salt	37

Sea Bones

Sea Bones	43
His Bones Alone	44
The Sounds	45
I come from another land	46
Angling	47
Beach Hut	48
The Sound of the Sea	49

Gift Shop Europe

Gift Shop Europe	55
Europa	56
Echt	57
Soft Bombs	58
Mother of Pearl	59

Foreword

Tessa Sinclair Scott's 'Dream Houses' ranges across natural and human landscapes with insight and vigour. In all these pieces you can sense the poet deftly questioning and testing her language, and because of the precision and sensuality she achieves, she does justice to her wide range of experiences.

These poems seem expounded wholly from both body and spirit and often attain their power from the way in which beauty and menace play off against each other. The style is fresh, incisive and this poet has an eye for complex personal and social milieus, finding imagery and syntax to match. Her work is memorable for the resonances and shadings she is able to generate through meticulous discrimination, and I alert readers to such poems as 'Dream Houses', 'On Arthur Street, in Onehunga', 'Europa', 'His Bones Alone', 'Sea Bones', 'Gift Shop Europe' and 'Soft Bombs' as fine examples of poems that are able to take the reader through sensation into perception.

So often these poems achieve a fine level of clarity without sacrificing complexity. The particularity of the observed detail is always balanced with the transcending observation, as in these lines from 'The Milky Way from the Veggie Patch': 'The Milky Way washes over us: two satellites cruise/ away from each other on urgent sky business.// Sweeping the high tops of the macrocarpas with our torch,/ we make mysteries for the cows in the next paddock.'

Tessa Sinclair Scott's poems are passionate but also disciplined by her careful attention to craft. A very impressive first collection.

Judith Beveridge, Sydney, 2019

Dream Houses

...que toda la vida es sueño,

y los sueños, sueños son.

Dream Houses

Our house, after the budburst rain,
after the embrace, builds itself over us,
while the stone takes root.

First, bring your heart.
Then, build a house for it: trample down the site,
peg and string out the base, unwrap the bricks,
smooth the paper flat.

Prise the roof from the floor.
Connect within, with without.

Build the house with strong chambers
to beat out our seconds, minutes,
to count down our lives.

Sleep loop through the rooms.
Swing on the door hinges.

Half in, half out.
Open up our house.
Lift up the lid, let light in,
Set honey out
And wait.

Green House

        Here it is—

        (deft,
        soft)

the bridge I wove from my own hair,
it's our turn to cross:
hand in hand, slow, steady.

Don't look down!

We pretend to be trees:
green bursts from winter fingers
tippity-tap tapping at each other's windows,
grazing each other's walls—feeding on shared air.
Breath by warm, wet, breath, we tendril about
each other afresh.

Our green fills spaces, hollows, dents, our bodies.
We rustle when we walk—stoop awkwardly to drink.

Light filters through us.

We feel our way along strings; the air plucks out tunes
on strings struck taught into damp black earth,
friable and full of the wriggling soon-to-be-dirt.

I thread these tender vines through your fingers,
wind them along your arms, plait three lengths
to crown you.

Light floods this quiet corner where we work
unspooling new shoots—stronger and more tensile
than spider silk.

>We build our house from words like,

>*Susurrus*
>*Osmosis*

>we are wet, slick,
>*just born.*

Purblind

Take this cup from the table, smash it to shards
and if you are able, throw the blue and white pieces
into the paint and paper sea. For we are the keepers
of many keys, keys to lock, keys to unlock—

an entire jingle-jangle bunch to keep time quiet.

Sleepwalk through the forest of you and me,
seek shelter in rough-cut huts, where the beds are too hard,
or too soft, and never just right. Escape artists, with small animal
tongues, we lick through sugar pane windows,
then we run, we run.

Take my hand to stumble under low-reach apple trees
to a tent at the orchard's edge. In the jellyfish jumble
of ropes and pegs, we lie above earthworms at their slow night's
work, mining citadels of dirt.

In early sun, interlacing leaves pock our nylon sky.

On Arthur Street, in Onehunga

In the damp shade behind the Sally Army bin,
the scarlet suitcase gobbles secrets, slurps
hopes, swallows dreams

into its zippery gullet.

It should have moved on, already be everything it can be:
an aspirational (just getting-through-this-hard-bit-right-now)
suitcase: but it needs help and it has this habit

of squandering love in all directions.

I scoop brush away the thick pink crust of Puriri petals,
slide my hands under the cream-lined lid, smooth open its flaps
and whisper into its mould bloomy insides,

roll home with me—let's travel together awhile.

The Zigzag Girl

Zick Zack. Snicker Snack!
The magic guy in a bow tie steps on stage,
in a trice, his singing blades slice her sequined torso
in two perfect pink grapefruit halves,

long fingers scoop out her heart,
hold the blood-soft pump up to the P.A.,
in the darkened theatre air, we cannot look away.

Every night, the trick is the same, yet we are entranced.
He spins the spangled cabinet, knocks twice,
speaks magic words. *Abracadabra, Simsalabim!*

A puff of pink smoke and our-lady-of-the-sequin-suit rises
from her sticky couch, like a pale bird picking across marshland,
she walks to the front of the stage,
arms raised in a storm of
slow-falling
glitter.

Now, tower

You cut out a piece of sky over Berlin, lay it
in a lozenge-shaped tin, put a stone on the top,
to stop it floating away.

In a tower-top room, I write rules for a living: I write
the day as a day, with sun, sky, clouds, rain,
then dark.

But down here, we run through the tunnel tipped tall
to climb a ladder bolted to the wall. Down here,
wedged in the point of this monolithic funnel
we are erased, and small.

Down here, you are nothing,
you are not
you.

I am nothing,
I am not
me.

We are nothing,
we are not even
us.

Secret Life of Stuff

The bed has a dent in it,
tiny us swim in an ocean
of our own brine.

The bathroom tiles are my bed now:
hard, cool, a balm for my tear-hot face,
a good place to dwell on your empty shelf,
forgotten towel, glinting diamond heart:
yes, it's true, the hardest substance
ever mined could not scratch it.

The doorbell rings ding-dong
it does not know you are gone,
the stairs wait for
your tread.

Sea Wall

The high sea wall of my heart
breaks, you
flood
in.

It is not bright,
or warm in here.
It is as cold as
kissing the wrong
mouth.

The sea clings, it says
I no longer know you. Says, I no
longer know
you.

A is for Aviator

Your bag strapped and locked.
You wait in an empty house.
Spring sun stripes honey floorboards
under tightly furled luggage.

You fly across a map of America—burst sound barriers.
At cruise, your ears fill with vacuum, and pop open;
like soft flowers for headphone bees to sup upon.

Window light curves behind you, a diadem of blue,
bled out to black. Language slips. New words nestle
under your tongue. Night falls from the wings
of the plane, drifting down at
dawn.

Burj Khalifa

We land
in a sandstorm.
My seat neighbour grips my arm,
points out the Burj Khalifa's tip
peeping through the grit.
Off to Casablanca on business, he says:
I imagine this is like 1001 nights for you,
I'm not sure what he means, but smile at him and imagine
standing in my kitchen in a jetlag cloud, watching the milk jug
judder loud to the ledge of the washing machine lid:
tiny sand, dirt, dust figures
swirl away from the eye,
to the edge. The
earth stops—
our clothes
part.

Paradise Diptych

Paradise Diptych

Peeled off McCahon's kitchen wall,
carried through the wet green of French Bay,
the Paradise Diptych hangs on brass-link chain,
from bolts dug deep in twelve-foot stud.

Over a square of monkish blue,
Adam grazes Eve's swerving curves.
Necks stretched and ready, they gaze up
at the scumbled sky, poised to cast their net
and catch four little birds
between them.

The Valley

The night wind drops gusts down the chimney.
In the morning, magpies canoodle in the megapine,
they queedle-ardle-wardle-ardle-doodle in the pre-dawn.

One good storm will tear their empire asunder.

At 3 am, the house tingles with silence,
under-floor fault lines unzip your path
from bed, to stairs, to bath, to the pantry
where rustling plastic trays betray
your night-time forays.

In the night I hear the river rise.

The fence swarms over dry grass to the road,
it unfurls heavy pine feathers wraps itself around
the compass points of the house.

This is where I learnt to build alone.

Pine Cone Owls

The metronome sets our beat, we run wild,
gabble and gallumph. Now we're slow-mo moon-guys,
moving to slower hours, just getting a moon-drink
from the *Raumschiff* kitchen.

Tuki shows us how to make pinecone owls,
at his workbench we hammer and glue. He says,
I hear a hum deep in the night – do you hear it too?

But deep in the night I dream only of cats
strapped to my chest. I wake in a blanket kiln,
your tiny arm baking me. Your damp breath
flicks in and out, it counts me down.

In the hut we are locked in, just one slender key
as poor protection from the night terrors:
they beat, beat, beat, at the door
of this small room on the lawn.

The Milky Way from the Veggie Patch

In the spiral arm of the galaxy, we two pins with cold legs
stand in the veggie patch past bedtime, to stargaze.

The Milky Way washes over us: two satellites cruise
away from each other on urgent sky business.

Sweeping the high tops of the macrocarpas with our torch,
we make mysteries for the cows in the next paddock.

The sky full of shooting stars probably deserves a mention,
but I think twice before putting it in this poem.

A Baumhaus is a Treehouse

A Baumhaus, is a treehouse,
is a house for Reuben
and Theo.

Komm Freund, sagt Reuben, *nimmt Theos Hand.*
Hand over hand they climb the ladder
    klettern die Leiter hoch,
ins Baumhaus, ins Blättersturm.

Leaves break around them,
a green tide washes the grey sky,
slides between leaf and stem,
zwischen Blatt und Stamm.

Jenny's Honey Shed

Over the 309 Road, we drive inland,
pull to the verge in a scree of dust to taste
Manuka honey from Jenny's Honey Shed.

Jenny stands with padlock in hand,
doles out ice-cream sticks from tiny pots
brimming with liquid the colour of wet bees.

In town, her daughter treads the dew-soaked lawn,
hums her body to ecstatic states,
singing to the bees to rise and swarm.

She lay for days on a white star-bloom bed,
until her shape was thick with bees, blanketing
her with a crawling queen's mantel.

In hospital slippers now,
she yearns for the hive's return,
as we taste the last of the honey.

Notes on Salt

We stop at Lake Grassmere on our way south,
to gawk at rocks of salt as big as rats.

The sea sits in a groove in your palm, a washed, pink, salt pan.
Behind the Nation's Salt Stack
the road whittles down to a gravel track,
ends in a wet, algae-green boat ramp. We've
reached the end, there's no turning back,
I slip the handbrake and roll us over
bone crunching bleach shells.
The windows fill up,
our lungs fill up
with ocean.

Sea Bones

There was no life lost; indeed, there was no-one hurt...they took care to put her on a soft place, and all hands got ashore without flurry.

Sea Bones

Tread across the bones of the sea.
Fold the map of the shining
ocean into your pocket.

Black rock glistens with
the tide's brackish breath.
Black rock cracks,
the head slips out,
the body follows.

Walk on the bones of the land,
bones blown bare, licked white
by carrion-eating wind,
hot rocks crack to birth.

His Bones Alone

His bones alone in the Awatere Valley, lie where he fell.

We don't know what kept him skimming the deep,
fishing for Leviathan, making the crossing.

In-one-port-Richard-the-other-Dick, was legion, he dove deep,
came to the surface to people the shoreline, seed a nation.

His island-dwellers eyes squint fathom-blue as what they see,
horizon gazing into the sun, without a sneeze.

He sets the course north; his wife hoists the youngest
onto her hip to wave him off from the wharf.

Bent over a candle stub, in a corona of light,
she stitches stories of the time before this mud life,
and nine children, and two drowned,
turned her young head white.

The Sounds

The Tasman Sea roils into the water, hoisting our boat
broadside to the swell. We wallow low in a chiselled chasm,
cradled in the wind's teeth — stopped dead by The Sounds,
we straddle the rip, where salt meets sweet.

In the Visitor Centre, the sign over the door reads
he tāngata, he tāngata, he tāngata. Postcards tell me
we're in 100 % Pure New Zealand.

From the viewing window, we watch waterfalls fall upwards,
skeins of white mist coil around supple black rock,
crystalline shards of our songs,
cut thru canned air.

I come from another land

I come from another land.
An island. It's a long way from my island to me.
The light hurts. The colours shout.
The roads are slick with carnage.

Possums, mostly.

At Nelson Street,
despite four lanes of merging traffic,
tailgating assholes and the sheer drop,
I glance out to the harbour, nod to Rangitoto,
before I swerve down the off ramp.

A boatload of cruisers from the acid north
lies at anchor at Princes Wharf. Come to look
and wonder how anyone could live
on an island at the edge
of the world.

Angling

All week, you plot precise angles;
lie in wait for the snake's chuckle
of the line unspooling.

All week, your pencil rules lines
from Gore to Bluff, you fill
 your filing cabinet with fish.

Out in the channel at last, the Kahawhai
run up from the sea to die on your blade.

You see into the churning green, you call them
and they come, leap under your knife.

Slick fins curve through the air
into the narrow trough of the tin dinghy.

Split from nape to tail, strung up with flax,
slung over your shoulder, you trudge up to the house.
Scales flake like chipped silver, cats thread through your ankles,
frantic for the soft, dark guts.

Beach Hut

Spots of gravel sting through velvet moss
on the overgrown track, the hut's rusted hasp
opens onto wafts of kerosene and brine.

The salt-tomb room glows mottled green
fingery shadows sneak across the walls,
flax grows in through the back slats.

Heave out sand-stuck nets and unwind green twine
wrapped to twigs and fixed fast with silver hooks.
Drag the dinghy down and push off through sand.

The curved flukes of the outboard
carve channels of white water, oil slick rainbows
bleed back to the headland.

Head out to deeper water now,
when darkness falls on the ocean,
sleep once more to the sound the sea.

The Sound of the Sea

The roots of the tree twist down to strangle through cracks,
in the seabed.

The branches of the tree rise up to graze wave tops,
above the water.

The heart of the tree holds a house,
with all-the-way-around verandahs.

Stuffing weeps up from soggy furniture,
landscapes scuff green-stain walls in silence.

In the maze of dry rooms,
in the middle of the house,
we sleep to the sound the sea.

Gift Shop Europe

We went to the ship directly we were called but the hatches were closed and we could not even get on board. So rapid did the fire spread that by 12 o'clock she was burned to the water's edge; and here we all stood 16,000 miles from home, in a strange land…

Gift Shop Europe

Last night, my dreams took me to Europe,
at least, a cable car and a gift shop.

We walk in endless heat down a broad, dusty street,
sit on steps to ease our shoes off.

Above us, a wind turbine turns, poised and reliable.
Its heavy whump heard only by farmers,
who wake in the night if it stops.

A crystal clear lake appears at my feet.
At last, a crystal clear lake, I think.
I dive in and float up, shadows follow me
like hungry sharks, I hover on the brink,
swimming as I sleep.

Europa

So, one day, you turn to him and go
Bro, we're roped together, like mountaineers.

Bound by:
the one-that-got-away, the one-night-stand, the-cheating-on-a-break-up-oopsie-daisie, the Facebook-crush, the work-flirt, the on-the-backburner, the next-exit-to-someone-better-than-you.

You drop this bomb, jump on the roof of your dream juggernaut,
show-don't-tell the elegant moves you use to avoid decapitation.
Nimble, quick, you surf out of harm's way.

But your bro is slow and doggedly graceless
bits of him stick to the tunnels, he diminishes, cries out:
I tried my best, but I'm from another dimension,
I struggle with compulsion…

Inside the carriage, hiding in the back row,
guards don't see you, afraid and alone.
This train is bound for Europa, there you hope, for home.

Echt

The astounding symmetry of every
thing in this northern flatland — no hills to set scale.

Long, low, endless plains.

The newsreader on ARTE has jiggly eyebrows:
switch to ARD and you will find no such frivolity,

or eyebrows.

For a time, I tried out flat & cool & smooth,
but it wasn't really *echt* — just the only way to mask
the panic of really being here.

Soft Bombs

Unexploded thoughts drop like soft bombs
or the second spasm of five hard loads.

This goes with that, then it's bingo: one of your ones
pots one of my ones, from a clutch of millions.

The moment life shot into me was a click
like a purse, snapping open to drop in change.

But the drain of these millions takes longer,
is less clear.

Mother of Pearl

This tenacious little itch
burrows into the lining
and won't shake
loose.

No matter how many
downward dogs
I do.

This lustrous single cell
is on a mission
and will be
born.

Notes

Page 15
Excerpt from Segismundo's monologue, close of Act II, in 'Life is a Dream', by Pedro Calderón de la Barca, 1635: 'that all life is but a dream,/and dreams themselves are dreams.', (translation by Andrés Crump). For full text see Project Gutenberg (U.S.P.D.).

Dream Houses
The first stanza owes a debt to lines from 'Gedichte aus dem Umkreis des Zyklus 'Eingedunkelt', published in 'Paul Celan, Die Gedichte: Neue kommentierte Gesamtausgabe' by Paul Celan and Barbara Wiedemann (Suhrkamp Verlag, 2018) (translation by the author).'

Now, Tower
A response to visiting the Holocaust Tower of the Jewish Museum in Berlin, designed by Daniel Libeskind.

Paradise Diptych
Inspired by the 'Mural for the kitchen of McCahon's Titirangi home', 1952. Acquired directly from Colin McCahon's French Bay home (now the McCahon House museum) by my father in the early 1960s, the painting, which still hangs over our dining room table, shows Adam and Eve in Paradise (to my child's eye, my parents in their garden).

The Valley
This poem is partially inspired by Denis Glover's 1964 poem 'The Magpies'. The Australian Magpie was introduced to New Zealand for pest control in the 1860s, and is now itself classed as a pest.

Notes

Page 41
William Haberfield's eyewitness account of the wreck of the *Sydney Packet* at Moeraki Bay, North Otago, page 9, 'Rocks, Reefs & Sandbars, A History of Otago Shipwrecks', by Bruce E. Collins, (Otago Heritage Books, 1995).

Page 53
Alfred Gann's eyewitness account of the wreck of the *Henbury* at Port Chalmers, source as above, page 18.

His Bones Alone
Inspired by my forebear Captain Richard Scott's obituary in the *Timaru Herald*, 01 December, 1882: 'Captain Scott was one of the earliest traders on the New Zealand coast in the days when visitors were few…(he) sailed under the protection of the great Ngāti Toa chief, Te Rauparaha.'

The Sounds
The words 'he tāngata, he tāngata, he tāngata' are taken from the last line of New Zealand's best known Maori proverb and were uttered by the female chief, Meri Ngaroto, in the early 19th century. Hearing of plans to massacre visitors to her Marae (meeting house), Ngaroto pleaded for their lives with the words: '*If I was asked what was the most important thing in the world, I would be compelled to reply, it is people, it is people, it is people.*'

Europa
The line 'roped together like mountaineers' is based on Robert Hughes' comments about Braque and Picasso, in the BBC series 'The Shock of the New' (1980).

About the Author

T.S. Scott © 2018

Subtle dissections of love, memory, intimacy and a fragile sense of hope; Tessa Sinclair Scott's work investigates these cardinal points with a clear-eyed gaze, illuminating quiet moments of potential and transformation, with poems of 'beauty and menace' in equal measure. In 2017, she performed the poem cycle 'ten houses' at the *European Poetry Biennale*, in Brașov, Romania. Those poems now form the backbone of this debut collection, 'Dream Houses'.

Born in New Zealand, further formed in Australia, Scott is a graduate of the University of Sydney's Creative Writing M.A., with further degrees in Painting, Design and Education. She lives in the northern port city of Hamburg, Germany, with her school age son and their nearly identical twin cats, where she divides her time between designing, writing and teaching.

Find out more: www.dreamhousespoems.com